TWINKLE TWINKLE
BIG OL STAR

Laura Norton

Copyright © 2016 Laura Norton.

Author Credits: Laura Norton

All rights reserved. No part of this book may be used or reproduced by any means, graphic, electronic, or mechanical, including photocopying, recording, taping or by any information storage retrieval system without the written permission of the author except in the case of brief quotations embodied in critical articles and reviews.

WestBow Press books may be ordered through booksellers or by contacting:

WestBow Press
A Division of Thomas Nelson & Zondervan
1663 Liberty Drive
Bloomington, IN 47403
www.westbowpress.com
1 (866) 928-1240

Because of the dynamic nature of the Internet, any web addresses or links contained in this book may have changed since publication and may no longer be valid. The views expressed in this work are solely those of the author and do not necessarily reflect the views of the publisher, and the publisher hereby disclaims any responsibility for them.

Any people depicted in stock imagery provided by Thinkstock are models, and such images are being used for illustrative purposes only.
Certain stock imagery © Thinkstock.

ISBN: 978-1-5127-6038-5 (sc)
ISBN: 978-1-5127-6037-8 (e)

Library of Congress Control Number: 2016916886

Print information available on the last page.

WestBow Press rev. date: 11/14/2016

This book is dedicated to my Heavenly Father; Maker of the stars, lover of my soul, and to my earthly father who generously assisted me with this project and countless endeavors in life. I am so grateful to be able to share this glimpse of love that would not have been possible without both. Additional thanks to some very special ladies: Fran Larkin Hyatt and Janet Donlevy Norton for their technical, and editorial expertise, and for helping to make this project a family affair.

Twinkle, twinkle big ol star tonight. Shining down on the one who brings light.

You've gotta guide the way to the baby in the hay. For He's the one that will show us the way.

Twinkle, twinkle big ol star above. Shining down on the one who brings love.

You've gotta go before to the one we'll adore. He'll be the King of Kings forevermore.

Twinkle, twinkle big ol star.

Baby Jesus, we wanna know who you are.

Twinkle, twinkle big
ol star so bright.

God made you to shine on
a very special night.

Twinkle Twinkle Big Ol Star

Verse 1

[A] Twinkle, twinkle big Ol [D] star tonight.
[E] Shining down on the [A] one who brings light.
You've gotta [A] guide the way to the [D] baby in the hay.
For [E] He's the one that will [D] show us [E] the [A] way.

Verse 2

[A] Twinkle, twinkle big Ol [D] star above.
[E] Shining down on the [A] one who brings love.
You've gotta [A] go before to the [D] one we'll adore.
He'll be the [E] King of kings [D] [E] forevermore. [A]

Bridge

[D] Twinkle, [A] twinkle [E] big Ol [A] star.
[D] Baby [A] Jesus, [E] we wanna know who you [A] are.

Verse 3

[A] Twinkle, twinkle big Ol [D] star so bright.
[E] God made you to shine on a [D] very [E] special [A] night.

*For a free audio file and printable chord chart of "Twinkle Twinkle Big Ol Star" email: lalala72@yahoo.com Be sure to type "Song request" in the subject line. You will not receive additional solicitous emails.

In honor and loving memory of Hallie Windham Hyatt (January 12, 1993- September 24, 2016), who was undoubtedly the brightest star in my life. Her life's song will continue to shine in the hearts of all those whose lives she touched. All proceeds from the sales of this book go to Westonwood Ranch (A farm-based learning program for adolescents and young adults with autism spectrum disorder and other developmental disabilities) c/o Emerald Coast Autism Center, 80 College Boulevard East, Niceville, FL 32578.

CPSIA information can be obtained
at www.ICGtesting.com
Printed in the USA
LVOW06s2303281216
519062LV00036B/183/P